W9-BIX-620

How the Food You Eat Makes You Feel

Jean C. Lawler

RED
CHAIR
·PRESS·

Experience Personal Power books are produced and published by Red Chair Press

Red Chair Press LLC   PO Box 333   South Egremont, MA 01258-0333

www.redchairpress.com

FREE Lesson Plans from Lerner eSource and at www.redchairpress.com

Publisher's Cataloging-In-Publication Data

Names: Lawler, Jean C.

Title: Experience nutrition : how the food you eat makes you feel / Jean C. Lawler.

Other Titles: How the food you eat makes you feel

Description: South Egremont, Massachusetts : Red Chair Press, [2018] | Series: Experience personal power | Interest age level: 007-010. | Includes bold words in context with a glossary and resources for further reading. | Includes index. | Summary: "Growing plants and vegetables and studying food sources can help children make good food choices, which is likely to result in overall healthier lives."-- Provided by publisher.

Identifiers: ISBN 9781634403740 (library hardcover) | ISBN 9781634403788 (paperback) | ISBN 9781634403825 (ebook)

Subjects: LCSH: Food--Psychological aspects--Juvenile literature. | Nutrition--Psychological aspects--Juvenile literature. | Choice (Psychology)--Juvenile literature. | Emotions--Juvenile literature. | CYAC: Food--Psychological aspects. | Nutrition--Psychological aspects. | Choice (Psychology) | Emotions.

Classification: LCC TX355 .L39 2018 (print) | LCC TX355 (ebook) | DDC 613.2083/019--dc23

LCCN: 2017948351

Illustrations by Nathan Jarvis

Photo credits: Randi Baird 17, 19 (small photo); Courtesy of the Author 24; iStock Cover, 1, 3-9, 11-16, 22; Katie Ruppel 18 (small photo); Emma Scudder 18 (large photo), 19 (large photo), 20; Shutterstock 10

Printed in the United States of America

0518 1P CGBF18

Table of Contents

Which meal do you like the most: breakfast, lunch, or dinner?

How often do you go food shopping with friends or family?

Describe your three favorite foods.

Tune In to Nutrition

What do you wonder about when you hear the word *nutrition*? Perhaps you think of eating, cooking, or growing food? Food is a big part of what nutrition means. Nutrition is about what you eat and how it works in your body and brain. Food is the fuel that gives you energy. It helps you breathe, learn, and move.

There are so many kinds of food to eat! You can choose fruits, vegetables, grains, dairy products, and meats. Eating different foods from each group gives your body and brain what they need to grow and be healthy.

Healthy foods have **nutrients** in them like proteins and vitamins. You can eat lots of yummy foods like whole wheat bread, apples, and sweet potatoes.

Treats like soda, candy, and potato chips are not good to eat all the time. They have lots of sugar and fat in them.

Eating a **balance** of good-for-you foods and a few treats is a healthy choice.

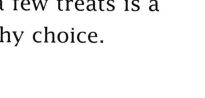

Food comes in all colors of the rainbow. There are red strawberries, green apples, and orange carrots. Yellow squash, blueberries, and purple potatoes.

You can use all your senses when preparing and eating food. Feel the hard potato as you peel it. Smell the broccoli as it steams on the stove. See the colors of the salad in the bowl. Hear the burger sizzle on the grill. Taste the raw, crunchy celery.

Food choices are all around: at home, at school, in restaurants. You may eat breakfast at a friend's house or have lunch at a farmers' market. You can eat dinner on an airplane or sitting around a campfire. When you play outside, you might drink some water. On the way home from school, you might snack in the car.

Fresh, sweet pineapple and frozen ice cream bars can be healthy desserts. A cold, sour pickle or a slice of hot turkey can tickle your taste buds anytime.

Notice how you feel when you eat or drink certain things.

You might feel sleepy after eating spaghetti. Maybe you feel full of energy after drinking orange juice. If you haven't eaten in a while and feel tired, eating a healthy snack can help you feel better.

You can learn a lot about yourself by **tuning in** to what you eat.

Chapter 2

Make Sense of Your Nutrition

There are so many foods and drinks to choose from! You could taste different ones every day and there would still be more to try! By paying attention to what you eat, you can learn a lot about yourself and your community.

Start by being **aware** of what's on your plate. Notice the look and smell of the food before you eat. Use your **inner voice** to connect to how the food tastes and feels. Eating with your eyes closed helps you tune in to what you are eating.

Paying attention to your inner voice helps you learn which foods you like and how the foods make you feel.

Paying attention to how food makes you feel is a healthy thing to do. Let your inner voice help you **be present** with what you are tasting and smelling. Notice how the food feels as you chew it.

You get **personal power** when you pay attention to how the food you eat makes you feel. This power helps you make healthy decisions about what to eat. It increases your feel-good energy.

You need to eat to get your fuel, but you can enjoy food, too! Trying new flavors can be fun! Experiment with some new foods at mealtime, if you can. Have vegetables for breakfast and pancakes for dinner! Maybe your family will join the fun!

If you go food shopping, pick out a new fruit or vegetable to taste. If you visit a farm, try a freshly-picked berry or leaf of spinach.

Have a good time trying new foods! A wider variety of foods can make mealtimes more enjoyable.

Sitting and eating with friends and family can also make a meal fun. It's healthy to rest awhile while you eat.

Perhaps you can plan to eat outside, picnic-style, once in a while. Being outside in nature while you eat can help you enjoy your meal more.

But being on the phone or playing video games while you eat keeps you from paying attention to your food.

If you snack in front of the television or computer, you don't notice the wonderful experience of eating.

Start a food journal and write down what you eat. On one line, list what you eat and drink, like cereal with milk, two pieces of pizza, or a can of soda.

On the next line, write why you are eating. Is it mealtime, are you hungry, or do you just need something to do?

On the next, write how you feel after eating. Do you feel tired, still hungry, energetic, or something else?

You can use your journal to grow your personal power. You can learn which foods can make your days easier or more difficult.

Chapter 3

See Kids in Action

All over the world, kids grow up eating foods and drinking beverages. What food grows in their local communities might be very different. But paying attention to nutrition is important to all kids, no matter where they live.

On Martha's Vineyard, an island off the coast of Massachusetts, the Island Grown Schools Farm-to-School Program connects kids to their food and how it is grown.

In this program, kids learn to make healthful food choices. They also learn to grow food and connect to local farms.

They grow food in their school garden, and prepare meals with a variety of local fruits and vegetables. They talk about their favorite foods.

School gardens help these kids see where their food comes from. They see and talk about what's growing in their community.

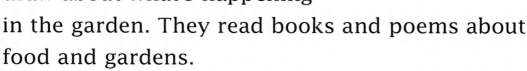

In school, they write and draw about what's happening in the garden. They read books and poems about food and gardens.

They visit local farms to experience even more wonder about growing food. Throughout the growing season, they harvest foods like lettuce, tomatoes, peas, and strawberries. They eat the food they have grown.

These Massachusetts kids talk about how foods make them feel. They talk about which foods help them grow, like apples, milk, and spinach. They discuss which ones are treats, like cake and other sweets. They are gaining personal power. Students grow food in their gardens, and some of that goes directly into their school lunches!

Moving On:
Taking Action Yourself

Get involved with learning about your food. Watch some cooking videos and flip through a cookbook or two. Mark some recipes you might like to try.

Eat some foods that kids who live in other countries eat: Russian beet soup, Indian naan bread, or Greek salad.

Find out which foods are grown locally each season in your area. See if it's different elsewhere.

Ask your teachers about starting a school garden, if you don't have one already.

Keep writing in your food journal. Learning to know the foods that make you feel your best helps build your personal power.

Glossary

aware: noticing or paying attention to something

balance: when parts are equal

be present: to notice what is happening right now

inner voice: thoughts and feelings you have in your own mind/body

nutrient: a part of food that provides your body with what it needs to grow

personal power: the ability to think and do things that help you succeed

tuning in to: to focus on something

For More Information

Books

Cleary, Brian P. *Food is CATegorical* series. Millbrook Press, 2011

Flounders, Anne. *Growing Good Food* (Our Green Earth series). Red Chair Press, 2014

Harris, Robie. *What's So Yummy? All About Eating Well and Feeling Good.* Candlewick Press, 2014

Llewellyn, Claire. *Why Should I Eat Well?* Barron's Education, 2005

Sharmat, Mitchell. *Gregory, the Terrible Eater.* Scholastic, 2009

Videos to Connect with Nutrition and Eating Choices

http://pbskids.org/arthur/health/nutrition/kids-action.html

https://mass.pbslearningmedia.org/collection/fizzys-lunch-lab/

Web Sites

https://www.choosemyplate.gov/kids

http://pbskids.org/arthur/health/nutrition/tips-kids.html

http://www.superkidsnutrition.com/sckids/index.php

Index

About the Author

Jean Lawler grew up in the 1950s when most home-cooked food was fried and most fruits and veggies were from a can. There were almost no fast food restaurants! She ate the same things all the time. She learned to care about what food she eats after the age of 50! She tries new things and grows some of her own food now. Jean thinks veggies for breakfast and pancakes for dinner are *wonder*-ful!